YOU ARE
TOO MUCH,

CHARLIE BROWN

Selected Cartoons From

BUT WE LOVE YOU,
CHARLIE BROWN
Vol. II

by Charles M. Schulz

A FAWCETT CREST BOOK
FAWCETT PUBLICATIONS, INC., GREENWICH, CONN.
MEMBER OF AMERICAN BOOK PUBLISHERS COUNCIL, INC.

YOU ARE TOO MUCH, CHARLIE BROWN

This book, prepared especially for Fawcett Publications, Inc., comprises the second half of BUT WE LOVE YOU, CHARLIE BROWN, and is reprinted by arrangement with Holt, Rinehart and Winston, Inc.

Fifteenth Fawcett Crest printing, May 1969

Published by Fawcett World Library,
67 West 44th Street, New York, New York 10036.
Printed in the United States of America.

THE WORLD IS FILLED WITH HATRED!

DO YOU REALLY THINK THAT'S TRUE, CHARLIE BROWN?

I KNOW IT'S TRUE..

THE WHOLE WORLD HATES ME!

"PIG-PEN" IS THE ONLY PERSON I KNOW WHO CAN GET DIRTY WALKING IN A SNOWSTORM!

NO NAPKIN!

SCHULZ